Texas As I See It

An intentionally, but only slightly, twisted view of The Lone Star State

Best Wishes

[signature]

Texas As I See It

An intentionally, but only slightly, twisted view
of The Lone Star State

Warren Paul Harris

Texas As I See It
An Intentionally, But Only Slightly, Twisted View of The Lone Star State

The Small Press
16250 Knoll Trail Drive, Suite 205
Dallas, Texas 75248
www.BBSmallPress.com
(972) 381-0009

ISBN 978-1-612547-84-8

Library of Congress Control Number 2011935164

Printed in the United States of America
10 9 8 7 6 5 4 3 2 1

For more information, please visit www.WarrenHarris.net.

For Karen, whose patience, support, and unconditional love enable me to pursue my dreams.

TABLE OF CONTENTS

Bluebonnets Through a Fence
Ennis, Texas
April 2007
Everyone photographs the Bluebonnets
in Texas. I suppose I do too. I wanted
something a little different.

Butterfly on a Harley
Frisco, Texas
July 2007

I had been photographing an old, rusted gate and packed my cameras in my saddlebags when I noticed this little guy on my handlebar. I quickly grabbed the camera with an ultra-wide-angle lens and took nine photos from every possible angle—at about three inches away. He never moved. Even after I packed up my cameras for the second time, he was content to sit on my handlebar. A biker at heart, I guess.

Survivor
Frisco, Texas
February 2007

While photographing a water tower in a snowstorm, I noticed this bed of pansies, wilting under Mother Nature's winter onslaught. All but one. This lone blossom seems determined to survive, even under the adverse conditions withering his neighbors.

Flora and Fauna

Ice Plant
Frisco, Texas
January 2007
Sometimes we need look no farther than our own front yard to find inspiration and beauty.
During the 2007 ice storm, I found this ice-encrusted plant, not fifteen feet from my front door.

Strange Brew
Barnhart, Texas
May 2010

This gnarly old tree in front of an abandoned small house caught my attention.

Upon processing the image, my usual vivid, highly-detailed style just did not convey the energy that attracted me to this scene originally. Monochrome seemed appropriate to this particular image.

Winston
Frisco, Texas
May 2010

It's not every day you get to see a baby mockingbird up close and personal, but Mother's Day is not like every other day, apparently in more ways than I thought. This little guy had been hiding under my daughter's car. After she left, I spotted him with mom fluttering around the eaves, hollering for him to run and for me to get away from her baby. Quickly grabbing a camera, I got off a couple of dozen shots with him all the time glaring at me just like this. He and his mom live in our yard and serenade us daily.

Tyler Roses
Tyler, Texas
April 2008

The rose gardens in Tyler,
Texas, are remarkable,
especially considering
how difficult it is to raise
some varieties in the
Texas climate. These are
examples of an illustrative
technique I like to use on
some images.

Three Longhorns
Crossroads, Texas
March 2011

A photo of longhorns was one of the last images I needed for this book. What book on Texas could possibly be complete without our signature longhorn cattle? I was planning a trip to a certain location for precisely this purpose, when I passed these three in exactly this position while out on the Harley one morning. I had to meet someone so there was no time to stop, but I returned with my friend in tow, not twenty minutes later and they had not moved an inch!

Zion Mockingbird
Frisco, Texas
February 2007

I noticed this little guy flitting around the tombstones while photographing the cemetery one winter morning and captured this shot from half way across the cemetery.

Peaceful Interlude
Denison, Texas
April 2009

While photographing a large cemetery in search of a particular monument, I spotted this flycatcher far across the cemetery. It was an overcast day and I was shooting at ISO 200, hand-held with an 18-200 zoom. Zoomed all the way in to get the highest resolution image, I took two shots, then tried to get closer for a better vantage point.

This was when he took flight. I was concerned that I would have motion blur or bad focus. Fortunately, this shot turned out very sharp.

Go Pigeons
Plano, Texas
November 2007

I spotted these two pigeons keeping watch from a neon sign when leaving work one day. I stopped, rolled down the window in my car, and fired off a couple of shots. When I drove closer for a better vantage point, they both made a hasty retreat. There are few second chances with wildlife.

Winter Bird
Frisco, Texas
January 2007

Standing in a parking lot in a winter snowstorm, I spotted this little guy, perched in a bare tree, fluffed up against the cold.

Final Destination
Plano, Texas
July 2007

Just finishing some shopping, I found this little guy embedded in the radiator of my car.
I felt it my duty to immortalize this beautiful butterfly, since my vehicle was his final destination.

San Antonio Squirrel
San Antonio, Texas
March 2008

I must have watched this busy squirrel for five minutes before I finally got this shot.

Water Lily
Ben Wheeler, Texas
April 2008

We came across this pond in a rural area
off a county road near Ben Wheeler, Texas.
It was full of water lilies and other colorful plants.

A Man and His Dog
Frisco, Texas
June 2008

While photographing an outdoor concert, I noticed this man
interacting with his "best friend." I waited several minutes to
capture this special moment.

Abandoned Gunter 1
Gunter, Texas
September 2008

This remains one of my favorite abandoned houses. It no longer exists as it was used by the local fire department for training a few years ago.

Desolate

(Abandoned buildings, vehicles, and the like)

Another photographer pointed out my desolation theme a few years ago. I hadn't noticed and had not categorized my work at that time, and his insight and advice made a difference in how I organized my work. This also helped me to focus my energies in certain directions and away from others. I have no idea what attracts me to these desolate locations, but it remains one of my favorite themes.

HDR Lumberyard
Whitewright, Texas
September 2008

I don't shoot a lot of HDR, but this composition needed the shadow detail, coupled with information in the clouds that only HDR can achieve.

House in the Woods
Frisco, Texas
July 2010

Exploring one day, I was driving along a gravel county road dotted with mobile homes, when I spotted this abandoned house.

Swing Set on the Porch
Tioga, Texas
September 2007

This house had been "on my list" for some time when I finally stopped the Harley near it one afternoon and took this shot.
Driving away, I noticed a satellite dish on the other side. . . .

Dayton Tires
Collinsville, Texas
March 2009

I love this old service station. If you look
closely, you can see two old men sitting,
rocking, and discussing the weather.

No More Soft Serve
Celina, Texas
March 2007

This old Dairy Queen has been exactly like
this since we moved to the area in 1999.
For years I wanted to photograph it and
finally did in 2007.

Split Cushion
Lameta, Texas
September 2010

This muddy, rusted chair with a
split cushion sits on the porch of an
abandoned business in a rural
small town north of Austin.

POW Water Tower
Princeton, Texas
April 2009

Miles away in the distance, I spotted this
water tower poking out above the trees
and decided to investigate. Imagine my
surprise to discover it was from an old
WWII POW camp.

Diesel Tire Repair
Penwell, Texas
May 2010

On a road trip to El Paso, I discovered the abandoned carcasses of the businesses that once had been vibrant contributors to the Penwell, Texas, economy. This long-forgotten intersection on Interstate 20 in West Texas stands as a fading reminder of our current economic condition.

Hillside Motel
Lameta, Texas
September 2010

I cannot quantify exactly what it is about
abandoned motels and their signs
that fascinates me, but here is a prime
example of one of my favorite images
from this particular genre.

Kountry Korner
Weatherford, Texas
July 2010

This falling down gas station and convenience store was most likely a bustling center of activity on weekday mornings.

Grand Rapids Furniture Co.
San Antonio, Texas
March 2008

One of the interesting vignettes of San Antonio visible from our hotel window on the River Walk is this aging painted sign on the side of brick building.

Signs of Abandonment
Mineral Wells, Texas
July 2010

Clockwise from Left: Japanese Auto Repair / Central Hotel / Peeling Paint / The Baker Hotel.

Grain Elevators Looking Up
Celina, Texas
July 2010

Now used only as a means of expression for teenagers and disenfranchised young adults,
these towering grain elevators were once a vital force in a once-thriving farming community.

Farmall
Celina, Texas
October 2008

A rusted Farmall tractor sits rotting away after years of service.

Out of Service
Celina, Texas
October 2008

A railroad track switch in rural North Texas.

No Riders
Little Elm, Texas
June 2007

I found this abandoned, yet fully functional trolley car in an empty lot on my way back from photographing a cemetery one Sunday. The light wasn't quite "right" so I came back the next day, found the owner of this oddity, learned its history, and photographed it in a much better light.

Quonset Hut
Celina, Texas
March 2007

A rusted Quonset hut sits near Preston
Road, just south of Celina.

Pignet Flour Mill
Gainesville, Texas
March 2009

An enormous old flour mill sits abandoned
and decaying in Gainesville, Texas.

Studebaker Wrecker
Weatherford, Texas
July 2010

A classic, old Studebaker pickup with Wrecker conversion sits rusted and slowly decaying outside Weatherford, Texas. An interesting trait of this vintage truck is the vacuum-powered windshield wipers. The harder you accelerate, the slower the wipers move. Not a lot of fun in a heavy rainstorm. . . .

Studebaker Repairs
Weatherford, Texas
July 2010

An abandoned Studebaker repair facility
outside Weatherford.

Studebaker Lark
Weatherford, Texas
July 2010

This particular model of Studebaker has a
special place in my memories, as it was
the first car I ever drove—at the age of ten.

The Chair
Possum Kingdom Lake, Texas
July 2010

This compact, rotting, long-forgotten chair sits outside an equally-forgotten business. Short and squat, it reminds me of a toad, waiting for an unwary morsel to flit by.

The Joker
Interstate 20, Texas
May 2010

A long-abandoned cafe on Interstate 20 in West Texas, The Joker sits faded and desolate, a stark reminder of better days. I am particularly fond of the arrow sign.

Assorted Damage
Plano / Celina / Allen, Texas
2008

Clockwise from Left
A tornado-damaged utility pole.
A trailer wrapped around a tree.
A small plane flipped during a tornado.

Wind Damage
Gunter, Texas
March 2007

I spotted this on the Harley one day, stopped, went back, and photographed this heavily wind-damaged barn. This was shortly after a pair of tornadoes wreaked havoc in Westminster, which happens to be roughly due east across the highway from this location. Coincidence?

Your Table is Ready
Valley View, Texas
September 2007

New Hope Cemetery: This table is over twenty feet long and it was the last shot I took when I photographed this cemetery in 2007.
I noticed this dramatic table, over twenty feet long and encrusted with lichen growth. I found it visually compelling and took this photo. Some dramatic
post-processing yielded these dark and ominous results.

Celina Ice House
Celina, Texas
October 2008

At one time, the Celina Ice & Cold Storage Co. was a vital necessity to this small farming community. When ice boxes were replaced by electric refrigerators in every home, the need for ready ice diminished dramatically.

33

Truck Stop
Interstate 20, West Texas
May 2010

On a road trip to El Paso in 2010, I found
this abandoned property with its blown-
out signpost to be visually dramatic. So
I found a position where I could see the
old truck stop sign through the support
poles and captured this image.

Cafe Sign
Interstate 20, West Texas
May 2010

On the same road trip that yielded the truck stop image, I found this delightfully decaying cafe sign. My favorite aspect to this scene is the classic curved arrow that no longer points to anything valid—and has no brightly-colored flashing lights with which to attract our attention.

Celina Farmall
Celina, Texas
October 2008

America
Celina, Texas
October 2008

Photographed in Celina near the
abandoned ice house, this vignette of the
rusted Farmall tractor (on the right) set
against the American flag says it all.

Rusted Pulley
Ben Wheeler, Texas
April 2008

Lantern
Ben Wheeler, Texas
April 2008

Hanging on the front porch of a historic
log cabin on a Texas plantation in Ben
Wheeler, I found these two relics of the
early settler days in the Lone Star State.

Shanzer
Gainesville, Texas
March 2009

This towering Shanzer grain dryer stands
sentinel near the now-defunct Pignet flour
mill in Gainesville.

Backlighted Silos
Prosper, Texas
June 2010

Scouring Prosper, Texas, for interesting images one day, I decided to investigate the old mill. I found an abundance of material there.

The play of light and shadow on the elements of this row of silos fascinated me.

Three Texas Trucks
Pilot Point, Texas
March 2011

This is one of those finds that caused me to hit the brakes, back up, and find just the right vantage point from which to capture it.

Dead Windmill
Pilot Point, Texas
March 2011

Like the Three Texas Trucks, this delightfully thrashed windmill, battered by the elements until it could no longer perform its function,
is something that caused me to backup and find the "right" vantage point from which to capture it.

Big Tex
Dallas, Texas
September 2009

Every year, Big Tex comes out of storage to welcome thousands of visitors to the Texas State Fair in Dallas.

Towering fifty-two feet above terra firma, Big Tex was originally created as a giant Santa Claus in Kerens, Texas, way back in 1949.

R. L. Thornton bought the components in 1951 and had them reworked into a mighty tall Texas Cowboy for the 1952 State Fair.

Big Tex wears size 70 boots and sports a 75-gallon hat.

Uniquely Texas

These are some things that simply "fit" here in the Lone Star State. Items that make a Texas-sized statement, or just typify this unique state. There is such a thing as a "Texas state of mind" and I strive to capture that wherever I find it.

Texas Star
Possum Kingdom Lake, Texas
July 2010

State Fair Cafeteria
Dallas, Texas
September 2009

The patterns of the ceiling lights and Coca-Cola themed tables caught my eye. Holding the camera firmly
on top of the table allowed me to make the time-exposure necessary for this shot.

Gunter
Gunter, Texas
October 2008

One of my favorite small Texas towns is Gunter (pronounced "gunner" by the locals). Gunter has had little growth or change in the last ten years, unlike surrounding North Texas communities, but it retains a certain simple charm that the rapidly-growing cities have lost.

Three Ceiling Fans
Edom, Texas
April 2008

Another obscure rural community is Edom.
We found an eclectic collection of shops,
restaurants, and architecture in this small,
North Texas town, not far from Tyler.

Texas Malt Shop
Hudson Oaks, Texas
July 2010

We came upon this classic roadside malt
shop en route to the lake and decided to
investigate further. The place was packed
with locals and the fare was excellent.

Transparent Windmill
Gruene, Texas
March 2007

I was waiting for my wife to grow weary of the shoe shop she had discovered when I noticed this small garden windmill across the street.
That's when the challenge started. Catching exactly the right gust of wind, coupled with precisely the correct shutter speed would yield the look I wanted.
It took about four or five exposures to get this shot, rendering the blades transparent yet metallic.

River Walk Umbrellas II
San Antonio, Texas
March 2008

A section of San Antonio's famous River Walk with rows of brightly-colored umbrellas along the water. I got the idea for this shot from one of my students. Hers came out better with more colorful reflections in the water.

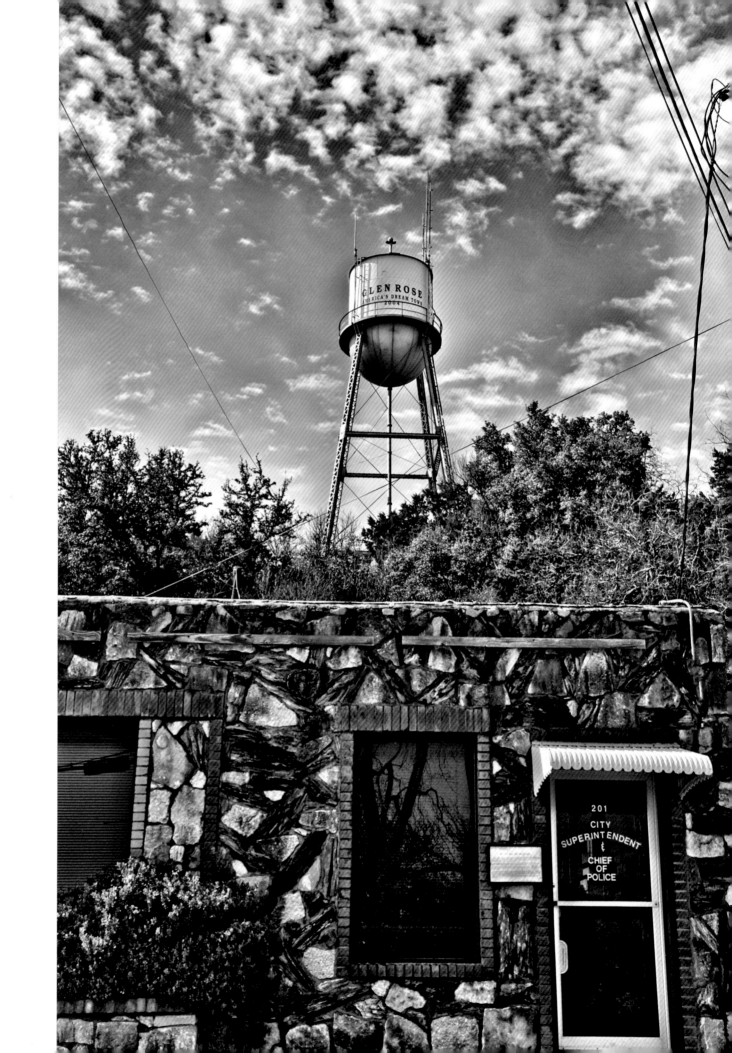

Glen Rose
Glen Rose, Texas
March 2008

Glen Rose is a town we pass through on our way to Austin every year or so. We had never stopped there until 2010, when we were in the area to do a charity photo shoot. Glen Rose turned out to be not only interesting (Dinosaur Park nearby), but has fun shops, good food, and reasonably priced lodging.

Lenard's
Mineral Wells, Texas
July 2010

When we passed this store, I just thought it was so odd that it needed to be included in this section of the book.
Used furniture. OK. But used mattresses? And look at the signs. This is classic.

Welcome to Gun Barrel City
Gun Barrel City, Texas
September 2009

We've been here many times since moving to Texas, as we have friends who live on the lake. Is this not a classic name for a Texas town?

Windmill in the Trees
Prosper, Texas
July 2010

In the middle of a large expanse of farmland sits this abandoned farmhouse, almost completely swallowed by an enormous, overgrown tree. Peeking from behind the tree is the windmill that provided the crucial water that guaranteed survival for farmers here on the prairie.

Rural Texas Birdhouse
Ben Wheeler, Texas
April 2008

This birdhouse stands on a plantation near
Ben Wheeler, I'd never seen one quite like it.

RFD
Ben Wheeler, Texas
April 2008

Driving through the countryside near
Ben Wheeler, I spotted this banged up
snail mail receptacle and captured
it as we explored the area. I liked the
brightly colored ribbon attached to
this aging rural mailbox.

Little Elm Water Tower–Infrared
Little Elm, Texas
May 2007

An interesting by-product of infrared photography is that it can turn foliage snow-white. This makes for some remarkable landscape photography.

Cross Roads Town Limit
Cross Roads, Texas
May 2007

Infrared image of the rural community of
Cross Roads's town limit sign.

Distant Infrared Silos
Prosper, Texas
June 2010

Infrared photograph of the current
(functional) silos in Prosper, Texas

Clockwise from left:
4th of July on the Lake / Lake Boats /
Independence Day
Possum Kingdom Lake, Texas
July 2010

The residents of Possum Kingdom
Lake, along with thousands of guests,
gather each year for the Fourth of July
community celebration. In addition to
the typical grilling, drinking, and general
revelry, PKL puts on a fireworks show
without equal. From the cliffs above the
lake, an impressive pyrotechnics display
is launched and boaters gather in droves
to enjoy the show from the best possible
vantage point.

Rows of boats are created to allow for
passage through the lake (albeit slowly)
when necessary.

Rowena VFD
Rowena, Texas
May 2011

A historic Chevrolet fire truck sits outside the
Rowena Volunteer Fire Department, with
the town's water tower jutting up nearby.

Hensley's
Collinsville, Texas
October 2008

Once a prosperous auto parts business, this is now the "wrong side" of town. The street is now on the other side of the building.

Got Jesus?
Denton, Texas
October 2008

Someone thought a park bench outside the historic Denton County Courthouse would be a good proselytizing opportunity.

Winters DQ
Winters, Texas
May 2011

I thought this particular water tower was really interesting, with the streaks of color and odd shape. And—a bonus!—a Dairy Queen nearby. A sure sign of civilization on a road trip is sighting a Dairy Queen.

59

Prosper ISD Tax Office
Prosper, Texas
June 2010

This little tax office from the last century
would fit inside the reception area of
the new high school with room to spare.
It has been beautifully preserved as a
historic landmark.

Dallas Confederate Monument
Dallas, Texas
March 2011

Pioneer Cemetery in downtown Dallas,
is the final resting place of many
historic figures, including a great many
who fought for the Confederacy. This
monument is for them.

Beer Barn
Watauga, Texas
October 2010

Apparently we are much too busy to actually get out of our car when buying booze here in the Lone Star State.
Therefore, a drive-thru liquor store was needed.

Pilot Point Bearcats
Pilot Point, Texas
May 2010

From the historic town square in Pilot Point, we have a view of the original water tower jutting
above the trees and offset by the town gazebo in the foreground.

Dallas Skyscraper with Longhorns
Dallas, Texas
March 2011

From Pioneer Park, a modern skyscraper
soars into the vivid blue sky, while a
cattle drive, frozen in time, makes its way
across a prairie creek.

Rangers Ballpark
Arlington, Texas
November 2010

Home of the Texas Rangers baseball team.

Cowboy Stadium
Arlington, Texas
November 2010

New home of the Dallas Cowboys.

Cadillac Ranch
Amarillo, Texas
May 2011

Shot at sunset in 40mph gale-force winds, this shoot was more than a little difficult.

Bagpipers
Denton, Texas
October 2008

Color Guard
Denton, Texas
October 2008

People, Events, and Activities

For an extended time, I covered local news, sports, and politics for several local newspapers and one magazine.
As a result, I was fortunate enough to see and capture some remarkable images.

Memorial Day Bikers
Celina, Texas
May 2008

Flying the Flag II
Denton, Texas
October 2008

From the same Firefighters' Memorial parade as the images on the previous page.

Flag Over Nastia
Parker, Texas
August 2008

Hometown hero Nastia Liukin, returns triumphant from the 2008 Olympics with five medals. A record turnout is partially shown here for her welcome home parade in Parker, Texas.

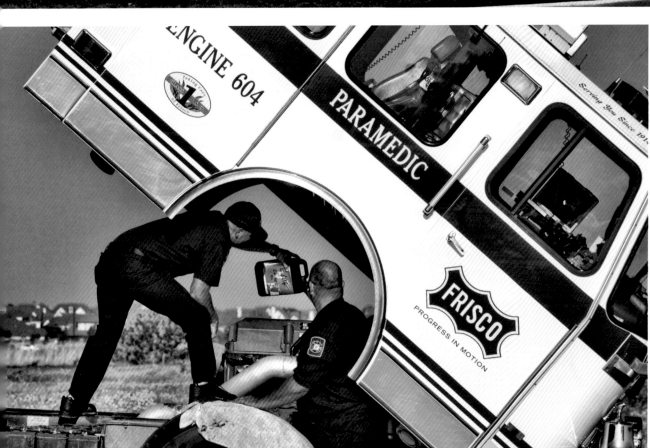

Pump Flushing
Frisco, Texas
July 2008

As we were driving out of our
development, my wife spotted this
activity on the other side of the car.
Grabbing a camera and pulling over,
I got this capture.

Truck Maintenance
Frisco, Texas
April 2008

Pulling up to Fire Station #4 to vote,
I noticed this, grabbed the camera out
of my saddlebags, got this shot,
and went in to vote.

Clockwise from left:
Watching in Infrared / Veteran / Old Timers
Celina, Texas
May 2008

Attendees to the Memorial Day
celebration in Celina, Texas.

Three Plano Balloons
Plano, Texas
September 2009

The Plano Balloon Festival is world-famous and brings both participants and visitors from vast distances to participate. On this occasion, I had arrived long before dawn to capture the "glow" on the last day of the event.

Conflict Resolution
Fort Worth, Texas
March 2008

Both images are from the Hillary Clinton
campaign stop in Fort Worth. Events like
this provide limitless opportunities for
candid photography. It is a singular point
in time where everyone is there for the
same reason, focused not on themselves,
and may be captured simply being
themselves under unusual conditions.

Mounted Police
Fort Worth, Texas
March 2008

Drill Team Girls
Parker, Texas
August 2008

Captured during
the Nastia Liukin
homecoming
parade, this
seemed like the
perfect image for
the last entry in
Events.

Central Park Fountain 1
Frisco, Texas
June 2010

Every image has a story. This one is no exception.

I originally shot this composition in 2008, as part of an assignment for the city. It was one of my favorite images. When I went back to locate it for this book in 2009, the master file was nowhere to be found. A total of about six images from this series simply vanished into thin air. None of my backups had the originals either.

So I decided to re-shoot this one composition and stopped by the park on four different occasions when the conditions were right—all to no avail. On every visit, all or part of the fountain was out of commission. Finally, in June of 2010, good fortune was with me and I found the fountain in working condition.

And here is the result of my two-year effort.

Frisco, Texas

Most of what I shoot is from Frisco, largely because this is where I live and where my studio is located. Frisco also has some unique and fascinating imagery to capture and remains my favorite city to explore.

Ominous Tower
Frisco, Texas
March 2011

I have photographed this tower on many occasions. This particular day, I was at my studio, just leaving, when enormous raindrops started to fall. Looking up, I noticed this impressive, dark, detailed cloud cover—and with a massive cumulus cloud off to the east headed my way.

I needed something dramatic between the camera and the sky to create an impressive image—and headed quickly for the historic water tower in Old Town Frisco. Arriving just in time, I managed to capture several powerful images before the sky opened and I beat a hasty retreat back to the safety of my car.

A "little" post-processing yielded this result.

Central Park Longhorns II
Frisco, Texas
June 2008

This bronze cattle drive in Frisco's Central Park is a favorite subject of mine. I especially like it late in the day with the sun behind the statues, as in this image.

Downtown Frisco
Frisco, Texas
March 2009

Shot for the Downtown Merchants Association, this was an "opportunistic" capture. I had made arrangements to gain access to the roof of a building to get this shot. The day before, we were coming down the street and I decided to try it from that vantage point. This is the result.

City Hall Sunset
Frisco, Texas
June 2008

I have photographed Frisco's City Hall on many occasions, trying to get "the shot." This is my favorite after trying every other location and time of day [night].

The Old Calaboose
Frisco, Texas
May 2010

View from the inside, at floor level looking out of the original city jail (actually more of a holding cell), known as "The Calaboose" in Old Town Frisco. The cracks you see in its walls are the effects of time on a structure with no rebar, as would exist in any modern concrete structure. Instead, the walls and ceiling contain random bits of horse shoes, bottles, cans, and assorted junk that do nothing to add to its structural integrity.

The city wanted to relocate the old hoosegow to their Heritage Center, but engineering research showed it would disintegrate no matter how it was handled. So here it sits.

Right:
A view of the little "pillbox" jail with the city's original grain elevators in the distance. Total interior space of this two room holding cell is only 120 square feet. Imagine being locked in here during a Texas summer. . . .

Frisco PD Infrared
Frisco, Texas
May 2007

I have photographed this building at every imaginable time of day and night, from every angle, and under every condition trying to capture its essence.

It's a difficult thing to do because of the facility's positioning on a knoll, and with the entry obscured by a sculpture.

Sunset, sunrise, 3:00 a.m., fog, snow, and rain have all contributed to the list of settings I have utilized in my quest for the perfect image.

Photographed in infrared at high noon.

Texas
Frisco, Texas
June 2010

A scenic view from Frisco Commons Park.

Station Six Sculpture
Frisco, Texas
September 2008

After this new sculpture went up at Frisco's newest fire station, I thought it was a very interesting addition that I needed to photograph.

I was waiting for exactly the right conditions and looking out my window one afternoon, I knew it was time. Camera and tripod in hand, I headed for the station (thirty seconds away) and captured this image.

Who Are These Clowns
Frisco, Texas
November 2008

We can always count on Frisco Fire to be at every event for first aid and some light-hearted entertainment. Seen here at the annual Gary Burns Fun Run.

Water Tower Through Trusses
Frisco, Texas
April 2007

This is a classic example of a series
of parallel lines that will cause me to
discard whatever else I am doing until I
have examined it thoroughly. This stack of
trusses, destined to support the roof of
a nearby commercial project, perfectly
framed a local water tower.

Sunset Fountain
Frisco, Texas
June 2008

I've photographed this fountain many
times during a variety of conditions. I love
the color produced by the setting sun and
it lends a special quality to this gorgeous
fountain on this particular spring day.

Clockwise from left:
Babes / Heritage Center Windmill / Frisco
Heritage Center
Frisco, Texas
September 2008

Highlights of Frisco's Heritage Center.

Cooling Off at the Splash Park
Frisco, Texas
June 2010

An exercise in contrasts, these
photographs are taken four months
apart. From the twelve-foot snowfall that
produced the winter wonderland to the
right, we go to a ninety-five-degree day
in June, where the kids are grateful for the
recent inauguration of Frisco's Splash Park.

Griffin Parc Fountain in Snow
Frisco, Texas
February 2010

IR Frisco Silos II
Frisco, Texas
May 2007

Photographing this scene in infrared gave it an aged and desolate feel. I was out shooting some scenic captures with an infrared camera one afternoon.
I had been photographing city hall and was slowly driving east when I noticed this image out of the corner of my eye. I stopped, backed up the car a
few feet, a few feet more, then another few feet, and rolled down my window. I shot six or ten images until I felt I had what I wanted.
A fifty-four-foot enlargement of this photo can be seen in the Frisco Senior Center where it is on permanent display.

Power Station and Water Tower
Frisco, Texas
June 2010

When I first noticed this power plant jutting up from the foliage, I wasn't sure exactly where it was located. It took a little poking around to pin it down and I found it to be visually very interesting. Photographed here in infrared, this facility with its requisite water tower is most impressive close up.

Frisco Trains
Frisco, Texas
December 2008

While teaching one of my impromptu location photography classes, we were exploring the Heritage Center and these two, long trains of identical black boxcars were parked on the tracks. I found this to be a very interesting vantage point.

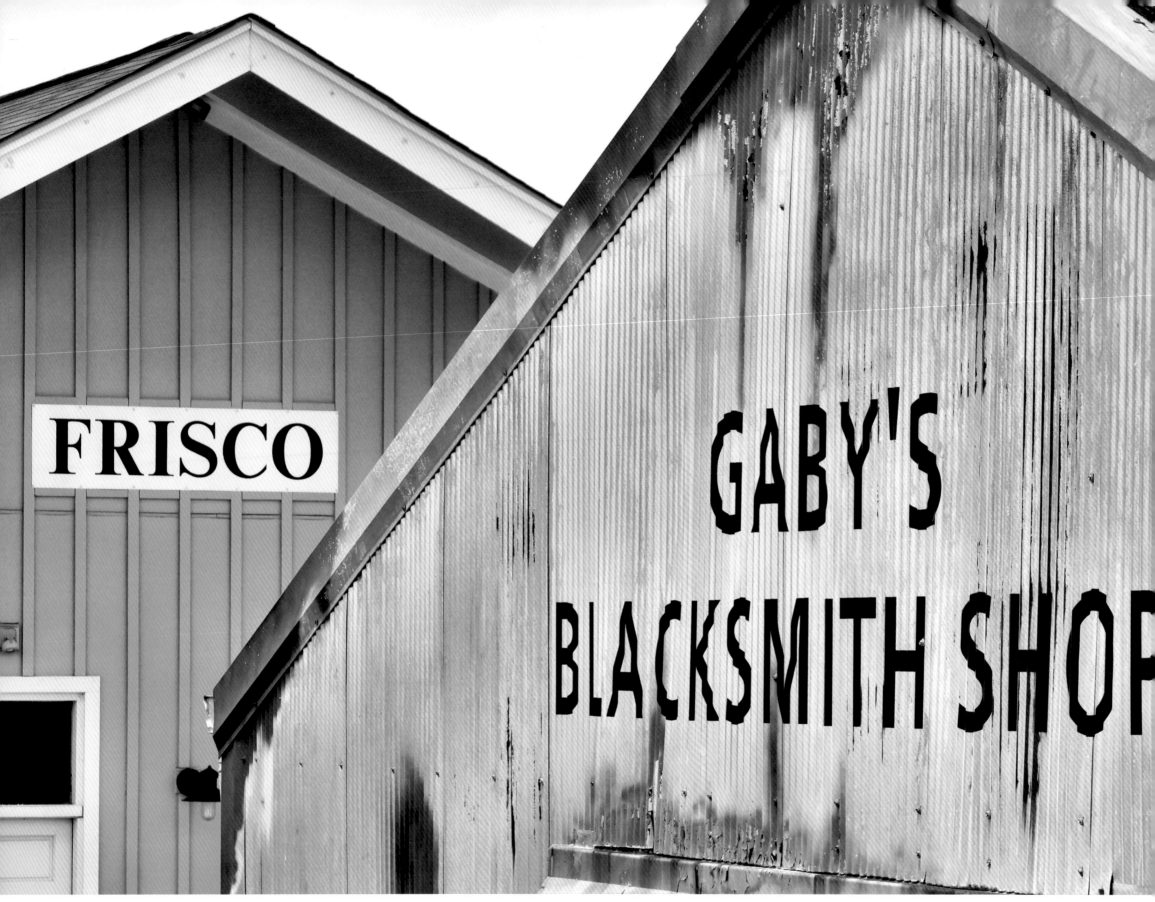

Gaby's Blacksmith Shop
Frisco, Texas
July 2010

Replicas of Gaby's (pronounced Gabe-ee) Blacksmith Shop and the historic Frisco train station in Frisco's Heritage Center.

Lebanon Church in HDR
Frisco, Texas
September 2008

Like many of the buildings in Frisco's
Heritage Center, Lebanon Church
was relocated from its original home
to preserve it for future generations.
Photographed in HDR.

Prairie Bells
Frisco, Texas
November 2010

Dichroic squares combine with tiny bells attached to a stainless steel tree-like structure to create the latest in Frisco's public art collection.
Located on the west side of city hall. When the wind blows at sunset, it is a very dramatic effect.

Unusual Finds
Texas has its fair share of oddities scattered about the landscape of this wide-ranging state. Represented here are just a few.

Bugs on the Range
Saint Jo, Texas
May 2008

One of my very favorite Texas oddities is the Running N Ranch, outside Saint Jo. On this vast expanse of land at a high point on the prairie, someone with a curious sense of humor and some free time has arranged not only this row of VW Beetles, complete with black polka-dots as if they were giant lady bugs, but also enormous flowers and optical illusions created with telephone poles.

Earthbound
Gainesville, Texas
March 2009

It is curious to see the top of a windmill
at eye level. As I walked up to this, I had
a sense of being out of sync with this
piece of machinery as it lay on the
ground instead of dozens of feet in
the air. This was the first shot I took but
walking around this oddity, I photographed
it several more times. As usual, the first
shot was my favorite.

Angel Tears
Denison, Texas
April 2009

We made the trek up to Denison specifically to find this monument. We were told about it by a couple we met in Collinsville the year before and it took a few months to free up the time to go search for it.

It was a perfect day with perfect conditions and I located this monument on the first try. With eleven cemeteries in town, I was pretty happy with the way this turned out. I was even fortunate that someone had placed roses in her hand already.

Decorated Wheelbarrow
Possum Kingdom Lake, Texas
July 2010

Two festive, unusual items I came across
in the very rural area of Hells Gate in
Possum Kingdom Lake. I am particularly
fond of the shape of this style of fire
hydrant. The Texas sun (and associated
elements) has rendered it an unusual
combination of colors.

Festive Fire Hydrant
Possum Kingdom Lake, Texas
July 2010

Gruene Lizard
Gruene, Texas
March 2007

Just when you think you've seen it all . . .
This very interesting business in Gruene,
(pronounced GREEN) Texas, produces
topiaries in the strangest shapes.

Gruene Monster
Gruene, Texas
March 2007

Lone Ranger Drive-Thru
Unknown, Texas
April 2008

We could never remember where we
were when we spotted this one. . . .

No Parking
Frisco, Texas
January 2007

This is what a parking lot looks like at the
beginning of a winter snowfall.

Trolley Car
Little Elm, Texas
June 2007

I found this abandoned, yet fully functional trolley car in an empty lot on my way back from photographing a cemetery one Sunday.

The light wasn't quite "right" so I came back the next day, found the owner of this oddity, learned its history, and photographed it in a much better light.

Storey & Clark Organ
Ben Wheeler, Texas
April 2008

Located on a plantation in Ben Wheeler, this particular organ is fascinating in that it is asymmetrical.
The elements above the keyboard are different on each side.

The Last Supper

This is an actual full-size painting, well-concealed in a building in North Texas. It took two years to complete by skilled Italian painters. I cannot reveal its location, but suffice it to say my jaw dropped after the door was closed and the lights came on. This painting is around twenty feet wide and an impressive reproduction.

Vietnam Memorial
Ranger, Texas
July 2010

We had no idea there was a Vietnam
Memorial out in the middle of nowhere,
until we came upon this in our travels.

How to Move a Horse
Denton, Texas
July 2010

Granted, it's not a real horse, just a bronze replica. But still. . . .

WTF
Gunter, Texas
March 2007

You explain this one. . . . This no longer exists, as it was bulldozed. Much to the approval of the citizens of Gunter—or so I'm told. . . .

MABLE PEABODY'S
Beauty Parlor & Chainsaw Repair NIGHT CLUB

Suite 107

DEER CROSSING

YING JALAPEÑO GRILL
CHINESE & MEXICAN RESTAURANT

NOW HIRING
BLUEBELL PINTS 2 FOR $3
OPEN 24 HRS

Curious Business Signs

Mable Peabody's is actually a gay/ lesbian nightclub in Denton. It's an interesting place. . . .

Chinese / Mexican food? Really? I suppose in Lewisville, it's OK.

And where, exactly, do you find a Bluebell pint if you do want to hire one? Just wondering. . . .

Multi-Color Spools
Frisco, Texas
May 2007

We were heading through rural Frisco one day on our way to some event when I spotted this array of brightly-colored rope spools on the other side of the road. I thought this was a clever way to pull cable on the utility poles, using colored rope to identify the circuits. My wife took exception to the delay caused by stopping, but my justification that "they may not be here the next time" won a reprieve long enough to capture this image.

Aurora Baptist Church
Aurora, Texas
June 2008

This really needs no explanation. . . .

Dino Rider
Glen Rose, Texas
October 2010

This strange roadside attraction has gotten my attention on several occasions and I finally made the time to pull over and photograph it in 2010.

Texas Birdhouse
Pilot Point, Texas
March 2011

Cruising the North Texas back roads with a friend one day, we came upon this old horse-drawn Grader parked in someone's very rural front yard.

The most interesting aspect for me, is not the rusting piece of farm equipment, but the fact that it has been used as a base for a bird condo—and to hold up a very large rain gauge.

Biker Dog
Parker, Texas
August 2008

During the preparations for the Nastia Liukin homecoming parade, I noticed this little dog, all ready for the ride, complete with goggles.

Carbon Plant
Big Spring, Texas
June 2010

Cleverly concealed behind the oil refinery in Big Spring, is this full-scale carbon plant. Literally just across the tracks from the refinery was where I found this interesting example of industrial architecture.

Collinsville
Collinsville, Texas
October 2008

The historic water tower on the square in Collinsville. About an hour north of Dallas off Highway 377 is the rural North Texas town of Collinsville. My first impression of this small town when I rode through on my Harley was that it looked a lot like any town on the Russian River in Northern California.

Architecture and Structures

Architectural photography was what might be called my first love. Seeing most subjects as a combination of lines, light, and shadow, I am still drawn to structures of all kinds.

Silo Detail 1
Frisco, Texas
May 2010

Close-up detail shot of a portion of the steel silos in Old Town Frisco.

Vivid
Fort Worth, Texas
March 2008

The colors of this building, combined
with the lack of a sign—and glass block
windows gave it enough interest to spend
a couple of minutes photographing it.

Edom Fire
Edom, Texas
April 2008

A classic example of any small town
volunteer fire dpartment building, right
down to the funky red paint job. . . .

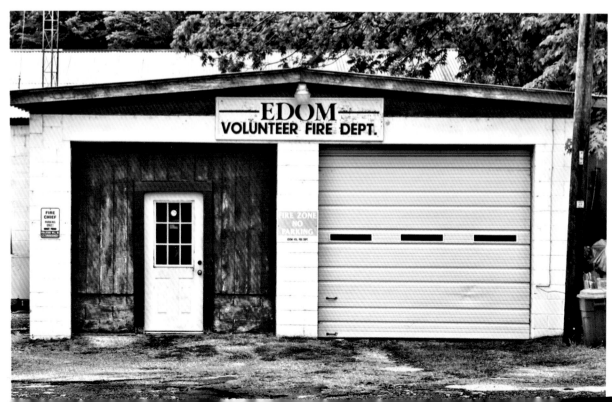

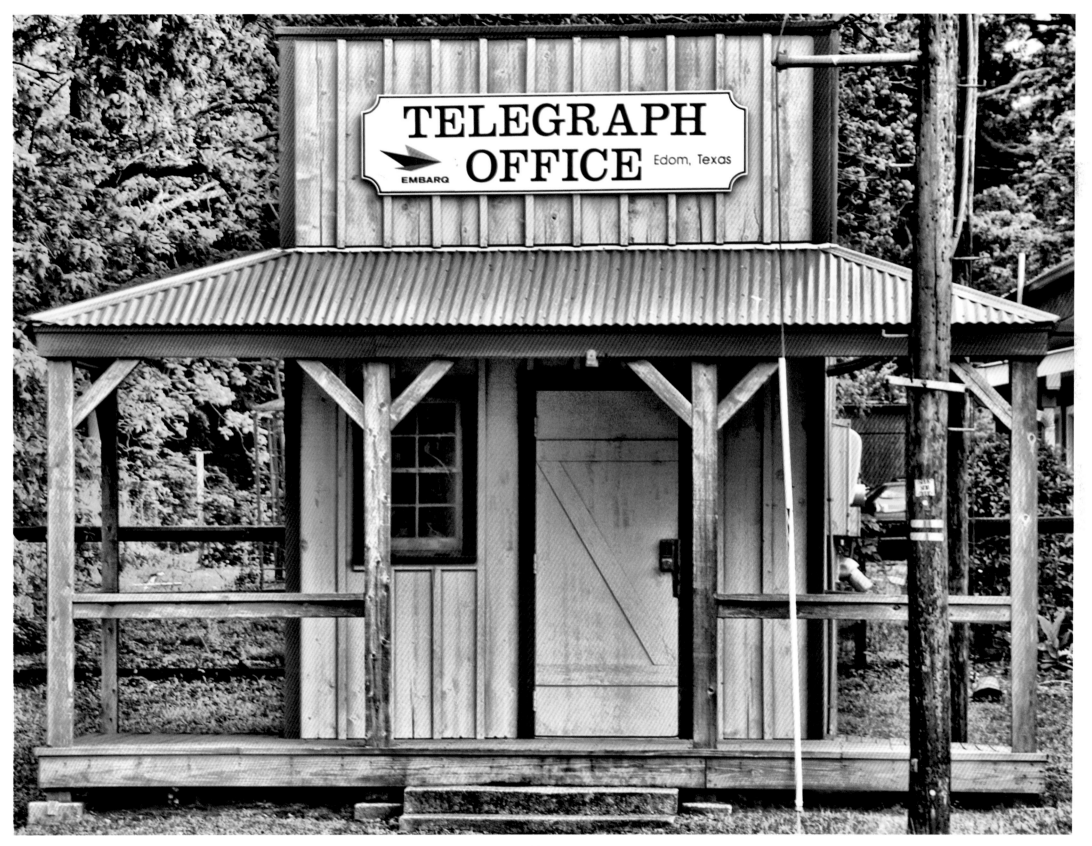

Edom Telegraph
Edom, Texas
April 2008

A beautifully-preserved example of early southwest pioneer architecture.

Will Rogers
Fort Worth, Texas
March 2008

The Will Rogers Memorial Center in Fort
Worth., is a multipurpose entertainment
complex of forty-five acres under one
roof. Comprising eighty-five acres in the
Fort Worth Cultural District, the Will Rogers
Coliseum was erected in 1936, along with
the auditorium and Landmark Pioneer
Tower.

The Coliseum was the largest domed
structure in the world when it was
originally constructed.

Reunion Power
Dallas, Texas
June 2010

Exploring the levee one afternoon, I
noticed this combination of high voltage
power towers and the world-famous
Reunion Tower.

Refinery Stack
Big Spring, Texas
May 2010

One of the refinery stacks after some artistic license has been taken with the processing.

Whitewright Mill 1
Whitewright, Texas
September 2008

It is my opinion that you miss a lot if you don't look up occasionally like small children do. They have no choice, because everything is "up" for them. We benefit greatly if we learn to look at our world like we did as children—with the awe and wonder that we have lost by all our years of education.

This fully functional grain mill is in Whitewright—in far North Texas. It is also an excellent place to go if you would like to see Texas from fourteen thousand feet up (skydiving, that is.).

Sunset Windmill
Cedar Hill, Texas
March 2008

I'd had my eye on this windmill for weeks. Finally, the sunset caused it to have exactly the right look. I adjusted shutter speed and aperture until I stopped the vanes with just the right amount of blur.

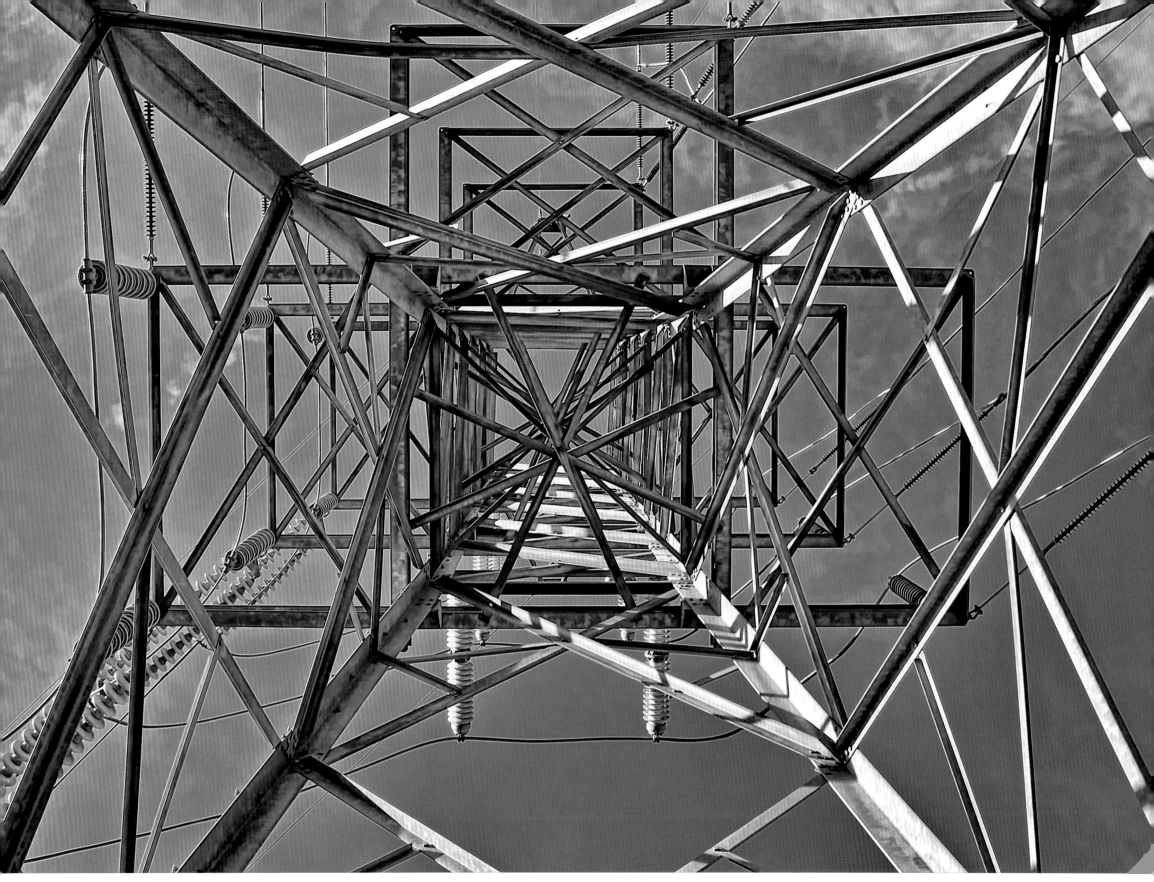

Power Tower Up
Cedar Hill, Texas
March 2008

While waiting for a class I was teaching to start, I decided to go exploring. It was sunset, and this high voltage power tower just looked amazing to me.

Pilot Point Bank
Pilot Point, Texas
May 2010

This historic building, just off the square in Pilot Point, was originally the bank. Now it houses a variety of small businesses.

Gunter Mill
Gunter, Texas
October 2008

This fully functional mill is the primary revenue generating source in this small North Texas town.

Dallas Stairway 2
Dallas, Texas
April 2008

An exterior stairway in Dallas.

Tower of the Americas
San Antonio, Texas
March 2008

At 750 feet tall, it is one of the tallest free-standing buildings in the United States.
It is eighty-seven feet taller than the Seattle Space Needle.

Dallas City Hall
Dallas, Texas
April 2008

Shot while on assignment for a commercial shoot, this is
one of my favorite Dallas images.

Old and New
Dallas, Texas
April 2008

In stark comparison, the old red brick courthouse
paired with the contemporary Reunion Tower.

Water and Power
Arlington, Texas
April 2010

I saw the distant water tower lined up through this giant power tower as I went by, so I stopped to get this dramatic shot.

Austin Tower
Austin, Texas
September 2010

I liked the colors of the glass, reflecting the ominous cloudy sky above.

Morrison's
Denton, Texas
February 2011

Morrison's Corn-Kits was founded in the city of Denton in 1886, when it was known as the Alliance Milling Company. The Morrison family bought it in 1936, renaming it the Morrison Milling Company. Under new ownership since 2006,, they still process locally grown wheat and corn into flour and cornmeal.

Cotton Gin II
Crandall, Texas
September 2009

The Crandall Cotton Gin is a favorite breakfast stop, especially for the biker crowd.

Denton Courthouse
Denton, Texas
February 2011

As seen here, winter is the best time to view the historic Denton County Courthouse, when the trees have all lost their leaves. This historic building was constructed in 1896 and currently houses the Courthouse-on-the-Square Museum. It is also the final resting place of John B. Denton, the county and city's namesake.

Vertigo
Frisco, Texas
May 2007

Looking straight down from the fourteenth floor of Embassy Suites can be disconcerting if you suffer from vertigo. We were here to photograph the Dr. Pepper stadium at night.

Scenic Texas

For as many years as we have lived in the Lone Star State, people have been telling me, "There's nothing to see in Texas." See for yourself.

Three Peaks
Nowhere, Texas
May 2011

In rural central Texas, these three peaks burst forth from the prairie and desert scrub.
They appear for all the world like cinder cones. And maybe they are. . . .

Brinkmann Cows
Frisco, Texas
June 2010

My studio is across the street from this large ranch. On my way to the studio one hot summer day, I noticed a small herd of cows seeking shelter from the heat under this lone tree. Arriving at the studio, I grabbed two cameras and trotted off about two blocks across a busy highway to get this shot. As I approached, one of the infernal cows sounded the alarm and they all started to beat a hasty retreat. Fortunately I fired off a few shots before they all made their escape. As it turns out, I prefer this shot with one cow outside the confines of the tree, looking at the camera. Cows are sort of funny anyway and this, I think, makes for a more interesting image.

Gunter Hay
Gunter, Texas
March 2007

We never saw hay wheels until we moved to Texas. I was fascinated by them as much then as I am now. I love this singular, bucolic image of a column of hay wheels on the edge of a verdant meadow outside Gunter. I spotted this as I went by on my Harley and came back to get this shot.

Frisco Hay Wheels
Frisco, Texas
May 2009

I found the stripes of color in the field, combined with the contrast of the sun and shadow on these hay wheels, to be dramatic and beautiful.

Canyon Lake
Comal County, Texas
May 2007

We stumbled upon Canyon Lake completely by accident. While staying in Wimberley on a romantic getaway weekend, we went exploring and came upon the dam that creates this lake. Walking across the dam, this vantage point seemed perfect. A pristine, blue lake is unusual in Texas, as all but one lake are man-made and are what is referred to as "mud-bottom" lakes. Created by the US Army Corps of Engineers by damming the Guadalupe River in 1964, Canyon Lake supports boating, swimming, and fishing., in addition to providing flood control and hydroelectric energy.

Power Towers South
Frisco, Texas
June 2010

Looking south toward the city of Frisco, two columns of dissimilar high voltage power towers march toward the horizon. The contrast between the modern, faceted steel towers on the left and simple wooden truss-based supports on the right is what I find interesting about this composition.

Green Gate and Chain
Prosper, Texas
July 2010

A dramatic landscape of Texas farmland, as seen through an iron gate, painted green.

Texas Landscape 1
Celina, Texas
October 2008

I had been on a search for a really cool old vehicle to be used for a client's family portrait. I had seen an old 1964 XKE Jaguar in a field, but it was gone when I went back to investigate further. I knew I had to find a replacement . . . so I took my friend Jose on a rural Texas photography tour one Sunday, and we found this gem just outside Celina. It wasn't exactly what I was looking for in terms of a setting for my portrait shoot, but it was (and is) just about the coolest setting for my personal version of the quintessential Texas landscape I could ask for.

Texas Landscape 2
Prosper, Texas
July 2010

Prowling the back roads of Texas for scenic shots one summer afternoon, I found this amazing old farm building
with another glorious cloudy sky above. This is heaven for me.

Lone Tree
Frisco, Texas
February 2007

This lone pine tree stands as sentinel on top
of a hill at Zion Cemetery in Frisco, Texas.

Tree Line in Snow
Frisco, Texas
February 2010

The last of four winter snowstorms
produced a winter wonderland across
North Texas. We were fortunate to have
this scene directly outside our door.

Sunrise on I-10
Van Horn, Texas
May 2010

Driving along Interstate 10, just outside Van Horn at dawn, I was witness to this majestic
scene as the sun rose through the mist-shrouded mountains of West Texas.

Morning Mist on I-10
Van Horn, Texas
May 2010

Just before dawn, as the sun is beginning to consider rising in the east, I came upon these mist-shrouded mountains on the south side of Interstate 10.

Prosper Landscape II
Prosper, Texas
July 2010

I found this scenic shot with a pair of trees in the middle of the landscape while searching the back roads for interesting images. I love the pair of oak trees set against the ominous, cloudy sky.

West Texas Overpass
Interstate 20, West Texas
May 2010

Depending on which way you look, you see two completely different landscapes. Both of the images on these two pages were taken in the same place at the same time. An overpass on one side facing north . . .

Interstate 20 Horizon
Interstate 20, West Texas
May 2010

. . . and a scenic landscape over the railroad tracks facing south.

Going North
Frisco, Texas
April 2007

Railroad tracks in Frisco, Texas. I had seen this shot as I walked across the tracks to photograph the grain elevators.
When I was finished, I held a camera with an ultra-wide angle lens down at arms-length, just above the ground and snapped
this shot. When I looked at the preview, it was exactly what I wanted.

On the Tracks
Prosper, Texas
July 2010

While exploring Prosper for scenic landscapes and desolation images for another project, I was approaching the railroad tracks and thought it would make a beautiful landscape to photograph the mill from straight up the tracks. Stopping my car right on the tracks (after checking both directions for trains. . . .), I rolled down the window and simply snapped this shot.

Abilene Wind Farm
Abilene, Texas
May 2010

Amazingly, when you get just west of Abilene, you find yourself in the midst of a wind farm that stretches as far as the eye can see in every direction.

Wind Farm Vista
Nowhere, Texas
May 2011

Bracketed by a mesa on one side and a small mountain peak on the other, a Central Texas wind farm stretches forever across the horizon.

Marfa Vista
Marfa, Texas
May 2011

Seven miles east of Marfa is a rest stop where visitors come to see the world-famous "Marfa Lights." Whether these lights are something supernatural, or just a drunken farmer with a flashlight and a hubcap, we will probably never know. If we had been willing to stay here for another three hours, we might have seen something like the "Marfa Lights." We didn't.

Highway Sun Rays
Marfa, Texas
May 2011

The highway between Marfa and Alpine in the Big Bend area of Texast bathed in the glow of late afternoon sun, filtered through dramatic cloud cover.

Dallas Skyline
Dallas, Texas
August 2010

This was the very last image taken for this book. I had been wanting to capture the classic Dallas skyline for over ten years and wasn't certain of the best vantage point to do so until making a trip to Oak Cliff for an art show in 2009. I made the trip back just before sunset in August of 2010 to capture this exact image. Subsequent road trips yielded a number of images that simply "had" to be included in the book. As a result, some other images were relegated to Book II. But this was the final image, with which I considered myself ready to produce this volume.

Artist Statement

In 2006 I had an epiphany that caused me to pick up my camera and reevaluate the world around me.

I realized I had been sleepwalking through my surroundings for twenty years. I had "seen" but not been "connected" to my world for a very long time. Some serious introspection resulted in the following observations:

As we all grow older, I feel we lose touch with the child within us and become jaded, missing the new, magical, and wondrous nature of our surroundings that mystifies and fascinates our children. Spend some time observing a toddler and you will find they are like sponges with sneakers, absorbing every bit of their environment, asking limitless questions of their elders and peers, and filing it all away for future reference. Every second of every day, they are learning new things and coming to grips with their surroundings. As adults, we tend to lose our sense of wonder, having long ago filed away everything we see. Now I try to preserve in myself the childlike wonder one sees in small children as they explore their new world. I consciously take the time daily to appreciate my surroundings and examine the minutiae that make up the world around me. With this viewpoint in mind, the images I produce are my attempt to present the magical nature of our surroundings in a manner so unique as to seem "new" again.

I suppose I see myself as half photojournalist, half historian, and half artist. Wait . . . math was never my strong suit. Is that right?

As a photojournalist, I'm trying to tell the individual story of each scene or subject I portray. Each unique object has its own place in the universe and a story associated with the time and space it occupies.

The history of our environment needs to be preserved and I find myself attempting to accomplish exactly that with many of my images, especially where grave sites and desolate subjects are concerned. Since much of this will succumb to decay at some point, I would like to do my part in preserving these objects for future generations.

As an artist I strive to create artistic statements and frequently resort to altered reality to convey the qualities that drew me to the subject in the first place. The essence of the person, place, or thing that attracted me to it originally is what I strive to illustrate via manipulation and creative control.

My influences range from O. Winston Link, Richard Avedon, Vargas, Maxfield Parrish, and Andy Warhol to the advertising geniuses who have shaped our culture over the last fifty years.

I hope my work moves you to see your surroundings with new eyes, explore it as a child, and appreciate your world as someone who has been given a second chance at life.

About the Author

"What a long, strange trip its been."

At the age of fourteen, Mr. Harris was taught the fundamentals of film processing by his father, who learned the discipline while serving in the US Navy during World War II. Processing his own film enabled Warren to explore photography with fewer financial limitations and utilize more creative printing techniques. While living in the Los Angeles area, he enrolled in a photography correspondence course in 1970, picking up some valuable film processing and printing techniques as well as learning composition and exposure through his assignments. He bought his first 35mm SLR camera, a Praktica IV-F, in 1970, graduating to Nikkormat cameras and Nikkor lenses in 1973. After the 1971 earthquake that brought southern California to a standstill, the widespread loss of power (and insomnia brought about by abundant aftershocks), encouraged Mr. Harris to explore time-exposure photography for the first time.

Working as a technical engineer for Motown Records and having friends throughout the entertainment industry opened the doors to live performance photography, which proved to be a natural fit along with his exposure at an early age to the psychedelic music scene in San Francisco during the mid-to-late 1960s. This, combined with Warren's background as a guitarist since the age of fourteen—and a roadie with The Grateful Dead in 1968 (hence the quote at the beginning of this bio), proved to be a perfect training ground for rock 'n' roll photography. He has photographed Sly Stone, Ozzy Osbourne, Metallica, Drowning Pool, Ted Nugent, Randy Travis, and 3 Doors Down to name a just a few.

Moving his family back to Marin County in 1975, Mr. Harris began his career as a recording engineer, working with numerous local and national artists, photographing their performances and promo materials, and honing his photographic skills.

In 1981, with increased fiscal responsibilities, Mr. Harris, as he puts it, "hung up his cameras" to pursue a more lucrative career in the technical field, opening AudioCraft Engineering, and operating it for six years. Needing a change of environment, he joined Symantec Corporation as a technical marketing specialist for three years before opening his own computer consulting firm in 1994, which he relocated to Plano, Texas, in 1999.

Mr. Harris credits an art class taken in Marin County in 1992 with vastly improving his appreciation of art and his compositional skills while confirming his long-held belief in an inability to draw anything recognizable.

An epiphany in 2006 caused him to re-embrace his first love of photography, acquire new digital equipment, and attack the art form with a vengeance, determined to make up for what he feels is "lost time." Never without a camera, Warren captures new images for his collection on a regular basis and has embraced digital manipulation to create his frequently dark and other-worldly images. In spite of being advised by a multitude of friends and relatives that "there is nothing to see in Texas," Warren pursues the obscure and fascinating beauty he finds throughout the vast expanse of the Lone Star State. Content to ride his Harley for hours at a time down endless two-lane highways, exploring the myriad small towns that pepper the Texas countryside, he finds gems of Texas history everywhere he trains his lens.

A love of cemeteries causes him to explore any necropolis he stumbles upon in his travels. Warren has been making a concerted effort to explore, photograph, and document obscure and historic graveyards that dot the Texas landscape as well as any he happens upon in his world travels; www.necropoliscreep.net is the website featuring these collections.

• • •

In 2007 a local photographer evaluating Warren's portfolio as a favor pointed out, "you have an interesting desolation theme going there," which was interesting to Mr. Harris, as he had not consciously pursued this style. This statement, however, opened his eyes to his own attraction to abandoned buildings, vehicles, and the like. Upon some introspection, he found it to be absolutely true that these scenes had always attracted him, which set him on the path to fill out his library of desolation images. A new project dedicated exclusively to this theme can be found at www.desolationimages.com.

In 2010 Mr. Harris sold his computer consulting firm to dedicate more time to photography. This allowed him to relocate his studio closer to home in Frisco, Texas, which he uses for commercial assignments, fashion and glamour photography, and a creative outlet for his own projects. He is putting his newfound free time to very good use traveling with his wife while collecting new images for varying themes. In development are two coffee table books, both nearing completion.

He has freelanced for local newspapers and magazines as well as international publications over the years. Warren shoots freelance projects for local businesses and government offices, participates in art shows, and has found a new love of high school sports through his coverage of these games for several newspapers. His work is on permanent display in city buildings, Frisco Square, Ebby Halliday offices, and in the homes of local collectors across the Metroplex.

Referred to as a "Renaissance Man" on more than a few occasions, Mr. Harris loves cabinet making, welding, playing guitar, creating various projects (his wife has a custom, lighted shoe closet to prove it), and is as comfortable with electricity and electronics as he is with woodworking, plumbing, construction, and plastic fabrication. As early as his twenties, Warren was an accomplished calligrapher, a skill taught to him by a close friend in 1989. He has done some acting for commercials, local productions, a Korean mini-series, and enjoyed a minor career in the voice-over field.

Mr. Harris was also part of the team that created the first computerized house in Tiburon, California in 1983, interfacing all the computer systems, security, and optical light collection devices. Warren also worked on the prototypes of the first digital 3D goggles while freelancing for StereoGraphics in San Rafael, California. He designed and built (or retrofitted) numerous recording studios over northern California, including MC Hammer's recording studio and custom home featured in several television articles, the home THX theater and rehearsal studio. His clientele included MC Hammer, Felton Pilate, Boz Skaggs, Randy Jackson, and Ray Lynch, as well as members of Huey Lewis and the News and Journey. He engineered studio projects as well as live performances at every major Bay Area venue from 1975 to 1992, when it "was time for a change" and he exited the entertainment scene for the last time.

A vegetarian since 1969, Warren is an avid target shooter (but clearly not a hunter), a licensed Texas investigator, performing data recovery and computer forensics for numerous court cases every year, and possesses a wide-ranging creative style as diverse as his background and interests.

Warren sleeps less than five hours a night, proclaiming, "There's plenty of time to sleep when you're dead." He loves to prowl the Dallas-Fort Worth metroplex in the wee hours past midnight in pursuit of dramatic nocturnal cityscapes. The site www.nocturnalvisions.net is dedicated solely to his Cities@Night Project. His wife has often suggested he open up a donut shop or get a newspaper route to fill his abundant pre-dawn free time.